RISING FROM
ASHES
TO GLORY

Finding My Purpose Through
Painful Experiences

TAWAKALITOU ALAWOE

Manufactured in the United States of America

ISBN: 979-8-9917255-2-1

Library of Congress Control Number: 2024925095

Follow Tawakalitou Alawoe

Social Media Outlets:

Facebook: Tawita QueenEsther
Instagram: @iamqueenesther8025
TikTok: @africanqueenesther25

CONTENTS

Dedication

I am dedicating this book to my mother Atsoupi Somali, my loving and strong older sister, Koudiratou Alawoe D'Almeida and her husband, my other sisters in Togo (West Africa), and my two brothers. All of you have been a powerful, physical, emotional, financial, and spiritual support system to me since our father's death. To all my nieces, especially Elisha, and my nephews (I cannot even mention all your names), sisters-in-law and brothers-in-law, thank you for being my family. We have been there for each other since day one. The unity and love we have for each other make us strong and unbreakable. Let no one or nothing on this earth take this away from us. Thank you for loving me the way I am. I really appreciate all of you for being there for me.

Autobiography

Tawakalitou Alawoe is a magnet on social media platforms, inspiring women to live abundantly by accepting who they are and being grateful and confident in their daily lives. She uses her past trauma and life experiences to motivate her audiences.

She is from Togo (Lomé) and has a Nigerian background and a Muslim father. She made the brave decision to convert to Christianity, knowing it would cost her both her inheritance and her status as a daughter. Soon after her father's death and recovering from an unknown illness, she moved to the USA in her late twenties. After several attempts at college, she finally graduated from Colorado Technical University in 2015 with a bachelor's degree in Business Administration, concentrating in marketing. This achievement made her the first woman in her family to earn an American business degree. Her debut book also marks her as the first author in her family, fulfilling a childhood dream.

In addition to her degree, she has earned diplomas and certificates in Advanced English, information systems, and computer applications. Due to her high GPA, she received scholarships and was inducted into the CTU Honor Society.

She currently lives in Denver, Colorado, where she works full-time, allowing her to focus on her writing career, business ventures, and opportunities to build generational wealth.

Acknowledgements

First, I am extremely thankful to God, the Creator of the universe, my Protector, Rock, Shelter, and Provider for paving the way for me when there seemed to have been no way. I am so grateful to Dr. Denise Nicholson, my book coach and CEO of Bold Publishing for her knowledge, loving personality, and patience in working with me, and for believing in my story. Without her and the Writing Incubator team and the other "Bold" authors, my book would still be sitting inside of my head and not coming out into the world. Working with her and being a part of her writing tribe gave me great joy, happiness, and much needed encouragement.

I would also like to extend my appreciation to Mary Beth Taylor, the Author of *Everything you did not Learn from Church: A Guide to Sexuality and Relationship,* for referring me to Dr. Denise Nicholson. Otherwise, I could not have taken that bold step to become a "Bold" published author today. I am so grateful that I believed in my dreams and goals, and pushed every day to get the ending results, no matter the time and sacrifice I had to make. Moreover, to all my close friends, thank you for your caring love and support, and for believing in me and pushing me so hard to focus on my goals and accomplish my deepest dreams. Finally, I would like to thank my family for their love and strong spiritual support which makes me who I am today: a daughter, sister and now an author. To all my spiritual father figures, thank you for your guidance and prayers.

Introduction

I grew up as the 19th child in a family of 22 siblings in Lomé, Togo. My life was filled with challenges—facing the chaos of a polygamous household, battling deep emotional pain, and struggling to find my place. Yet, through all the hell, fire, and tumultuous waters, I emerged as a strong, confident, and resilient woman.

This book is not just a recount of my past but a testament to the power of faith, perseverance, and self-belief. I share my journey to help others move beyond their past and realize that life, despite its hardships, is a gift full of joy and possibility. No matter how dark things may seem, if we trust in ourselves and in God's plan, things can change for the better. The sun always rises on a new day, and nothing can stop that.

I've learned that our past doesn't define us, it refines us and shapes us into the people we are meant to be. My painful experiences, from losing my father to surviving a coma, have taught me to never give up. Each struggle brought me closer to discovering my true purpose and becoming the woman God intended me to be.

In this book, I hope to inspire you with my story, showing that no matter what we face, there is always hope, always a way forward. I'm living proof that God is still working miracles, and I invite you to believe in Him, believe in yourself, and never give up.

Chapter 1

Who Is TAWA?

There were times when I wondered if I was born into the wrong country, continent, or even family. But I've come to believe that God doesn't make mistakes. We are all placed in specific locations and families for a purpose.

I was born and raised in Lomé, Togo, a small country in West Africa with a population of about eight million people. Despite its rich culture and history, Togo is often overlooked by much of the world, especially Americans. Politically, the country has long been under the control of the same ruling party, and though we're supposed to be a democratic nation, it feels far from that. I'm not one to delve into politics or corruption, so I generally avoid those discussions.

Lomé, the capital and largest city, is known for its palm-lined Atlantic coastline and cultural landmarks like the Independence Monument and the National Museum, which showcases West African artifacts. There's also the Akodessewa Fetish Market, famous for selling voodoo-related items like animal skins and skulls.

Though Togo is small, it holds a unique place in the world, and I now see the reason why I was born there.

The main language spoken in southern Togo is Ewe, along with 36 other dialects throughout the country. Togo was once called Togoland and served as a buffer zone between the Asante and Dahomey states, with various ethnic groups living in relative isolation from one another.

In 1884, Togoland became a German protectorate, but by 1914, it was occupied by British and French forces during World War I. In 1922, the League of Nations assigned eastern Togoland to France (which is why French is spoken in Togo) and the western portion to Britain. By 1946, both the British and French territories were placed under the United Nations Trusteeship Council. Ten years later, British Togoland was integrated into the Gold Coast (now Ghana), while French Togoland became an independent republic within the French Union.

Togo officially gained independence on April 27, 1960. Since then, its economy has largely depended on agriculture, with significant reserves of phosphate playing an important role.

I was born on Friday, August 15, during the beautiful summer when the trees blossom like in heaven, and everything is lush and green. You can even smell the rain in the air. You might wonder how I know all these details about my birth – my mother shared them with me, and I also did some research about the time I was born.

My city is near the ocean, surrounded by palm trees. The climate is humid and tropical, similar to Florida, and green like Seattle, Washington. I've always loved my city for its beachside picnics and fun activities. The people are warm, and neighbors live close like family. Everyone is happy, regardless of what they have.

However, I don't recall all the details of my childhood like some might, because it wasn't all glitter. My father was Muslim and a polygamist, and was married four times. All his wives were living together in the same house, under the same roof, pretty much like Sister

Wives in Utah (USA). Yes, this was permissible for Muslim religion and culture. My father was married to my mother who was the fourth wife, but she was Togolese (Ewe tribe) and was born a Catholic with Christian practices. My father was a very successful businessman who traveled a lot around the west region of Africa. At that time, my father was selling auto parts and was involved in a big truck business. He met my mother during one of his business trips. It did not take a long time for them to get married; my mother was an 18 year old virgin at that time. Being married as a virgin is a huge thing in my culture because it shows love, respect, purity, honor and dignity, not only for yourself as a woman but also for your family, especially since your parents get a huge lump sum called "A Bride Price". It can consist of clothing, money and expensive wines. This depends on the family you come from as well. My father was my mother's first and last love when he passed away in 1999 from heart failure. That is another long story. I missed my father's presence because he was a protector and loved us to the best of his ability, even though he was not always present physically, emotionally and mentally for us. I did not have a full time father figure. However, he wanted the best for all of us.

Who could imagine having a father with four wives with a busy lifestyle? Was life easy for me? Not really. I wore this mask everyday among my friends and family to pretend to be someone I was not. In other words, I faked it until I made every day a happy one. At times, I had asked myself how my mother got herself in that cruel life of polygamy. To me, it seemed she had to work so hard to get my father's love and attention. He only visited us when we needed monthly allowances and tuition fees, or if we had to ask him something in person. To speak to him in person, I had to travel in public transportation many miles away. My father was not just a polygamist, he was a very rich man who lived in the suburban neighborhood of Lomé, which is like Cherry Creek in Denver, Colorado. On the other hand, my mother, my other siblings, and I had our home in a poor neighborhood. I felt a disconnect, mostly because there was not much of my father's presence, and where we lived was very different from where he lived.

However, even though my father was not present in the home while we were growing up, he was there for us financially. I was lucky to attend the best private school in the city, which most children wished their parents could afford. So, yes I was fortunate to have a great provider like my father.

My father wasn't often around because he primarily lived with his second wife and her children – he would visit us on weekends and occasionally during the week. While he was a great provider, we received monthly allowances to cover our basic needs, so I never had to worry about money or food while he was alive. I used the money to shop for beauty products and fashionable clothes. That allowed me to style any outfit I chose.

I believe style is in my DNA; I've always had an innate sense of fashion. Because everything I wanted was handed to me on a silver platter, I never worked or took summer jobs.

My father's death was a wakeup call to my adulthood. This was followed by a mysterious, unknown illness which put me in a coma for three months. I was paralyzed in bed; this I will explain in more depth in another chapter. I cried and screamed from the inside of my whole being. Why should I make an appointment with my father when I was craving for his attention, care, and love? I asked myself this question multiple times and on several occasions. All I wanted was his presence and everything a daughter could get from her father: "FATHER LOVE".

Despite this, we had a house with no mortgage payment and our basic needs were provided for. Besides that, I wanted my father to be present spiritually, physically, emotionally and mentally not just financially. Growing up, I remember experiencing a lot of fights between either my mother and other wives or me fighting with my half-brothers and sisters. I was not happy even though I went to the best private high school in my city where all the rich or cool kids wanted to be. I was always depressed inside. On the outside other families and friends viewed me as the happiest girl ever, but a pretty smile and beautiful looks can be deceiving. Sometimes, it seems that human beings are wired to be that way, but it does not have to be so. I was just following rules and family traditions. I didn't even know the reason for doing so.

Out of ignorance, my parents had put us under, and bound us to evil spirits and demonic protection: thinking that was the right way for shelter, safety and provision. According to the tradition, the children born in such union are guided and raised based on the father's religion and willpower. My mother had no authority as to what the destiny of the family should be; Neither was she concerned because it is a misogynist world where men always predestine family decisions.

Since birth, I was raised a Muslim not knowing the ordeals I had to go through or face in terms of culture, tradition and rituals. At a young age, most girls are already assigned to an older man, around fifty to sixty years old to become their future husband at their father's choice.

Being in junior high school for me was permanent trauma, depression – living in fear because my father was convinced that the time had come for me to be circumcised in order to be considered for marriage. My mother, who is Christian knew that my life was about to turn into a zone of torment and woe, started to worry and desperately began to seek some help for my protection. She sought help from my older sister who was then a citizen of the United States of America.

My Family Background

I was born into a big family, not knowing the destiny that was planned ahead of me. My most memorable times are my middle and high school years where a cute, innocent girl was born in Muslim family with no goals, vision or dreams. I grew up in a very conservative Muslim family, where my parents instilled in me the values of Islamic faith. I had observed my daily prayers from a very young age, and maintained a strict diet, abstaining from eating pork products, alcohol, and other forbidden items prohibited by my religion. I had followed my father's religion because I did not have any choice. I prayed five times a day, went to mosque every Friday, and wrapped my head with a scarf with no questions asked. Being raised in a Muslim family had its advantages, but I always had questions in my mind about my faith that were unanswered. I longed for a deeper and more personal relationship with God, and often felt unfulfilled practicing the religion of Islam. I was afraid to ask my father the meaning of all that I was doing in my religion. There were so many questions unanswered in my mind when my father was alive. However, I did not get those answers until I became converted from a Muslim to a Christian. It was a bold and fulfilling decision. My father was very strict, and I was afraid to ask deeper questions about the religion of Islam. Plus, he only visited us every weekend or sometimes twice a month. I remembered we all would be in our best behaviors when we heard he was coming to visit. We made sure our rooms were clean and homework done. I remembered that my older siblings would be on the watch from outside of our home, shouting, "Baba (Father in Yoruba language) is coming, Baba is coming Be prepared!". It was not funny that time but I can laugh about it today with no remorse.

Most of my other siblings (half-brother and sisters) were jealous of us: my mother's children. The reason for this was because we were so distinguished in everything: education, beauty, creativity, spiritual gifts, money management, and finance. I can name all the reasons in one sentence: we were born with excellence and greatness within us. In middle school, I remembered wearing a long khaki dress uniform past my knees. My home was not far away from my school so we walked mostly on foot with backpacks filled with lunch and snacks that my mother always made for us. Our morning routine consisted of breakfast: oatmeal, eggs and fresh French bread made straight from those old ovens which used wood as fuel. I loved the taste in my mouth because it was always hot and freshly baked. In my country, most of our food is cooked homemade – We don't have a lot of fast-food restaurants like they have in the United States or western world. Family gatherings are a tradition where we eat together from one plate with different healthy dishes. Our lifestyle is a healthy diet, and I grew up keeping that healthy way of living even when living here in the USA for almost 2 decades now. What I have learned from this lifestyle is the importance of family gathering , and the bonding of family; which has made me a strong and mature woman today. It has caused me to value my background, cultures, and traditions. I have learned that unity in my family helped us to accomplish great things such as, building a new home for my mother a couple of years ago and taking care of her. As a matter of fact, my mother, who belongs to the Ewe Tribe even though she is Catholic, was forced to practice indigenous religions. My mother has never been in school. According to my grandfather's philosophy, girls were meant to be housemates and boys were supposed to be in school. He believed if women went to school and became very educated, smart, or brilliant, they would not respect their men or husbands. It is a misogynistic society where men are leaders, providers, breadwinners and protectors and women are to be home doing their duties like cooking, cleaning, making children and taking care of their husbands' needs: bathing and sex. In fact, my parents got married despite the difference of their cultures and religions. My father never pressured her to become the perfect Muslim wife or converted her. I can not imagine the backlash they had to face from family and people because of their marriage. This was not actually about race or ethnicity, it was actually about tribe, religion and cultural differences. In spite of everything, my mother became the fourth wife of my father. I did not know much of what happened during their marriage before I was born, but this one thing I do know: my mother did not have a happy marriage before or after my birth. My mother was a housewife who had her own small business selling charcoal for cooking. She supplied the entire neighborhood and her loyal customers ordered wholesale. My mother was a strong woman who never gave up on us. I could describe her as the Proverbs 31 Woman. Her small business was a backup for us when my father's allowances came in late or were delayed. I have learned a lot from my mother: cooking, cleaning, and organizing my rooms – making sure everything was clean and neat. I recall that I was happy every day, always with a smile, ready to be in school and ready to learn. I loved to read books and write poems at a young age. I was involved in the performing arts: acting, singing, and dancing classes as extracurricular activities. I joined the girls' soccer team when I was in middle school because football back home is everyone's favorite sport. I was at the top of my class. My teachers would choose me to supervise my classmates when they were in meetings with the director, other teachers, or when they took their breaks. I was the smartest girl in most of my classes. I never failed any class from primary school until I graduated from high school. I was a good girl in the family, but inside I had a noncompliant spirit which would come out occasionally. I was never involved in school fights or any violent activities except for one encounter I had with a tall boy who used to bully me and my friend after school.

When I graduated from middle school, I told my father that I wanted to go to the best private high school in town. I registered at Polytechnique Bruce high school; it was owned by a second generation of German families. There are a lot of first to third generation Germans in my country: back in World War I, Germans colonized my country, and after World War II it was invaded by the British and French. After several battles, the French took over, hence the reason why I speak French. When I was six years old, I started learning French, which is our main spoken language in school. My main language however, is Ewe. From my personal opinion and experiences, colonization has positive and negative aspects. However, I never grew up focusing on the negative aspect as much as some people do. I focus on the positive aspect of this, which is that I speak fluent French and learn some of the western world's culture.

I could describe my high school as mostly dominated by rich suburban kids who were trying to impress their friends and other families who could not afford it. I was smart, intelligent, and brilliant: the most favorite and attractive student in all my classes. Often I would get a lunch invitation to eat with my friends, or an invitation to eat with my teachers in their big mansions. That had caused a lot of jealousy among my fellow classmates. They were saying that my grades were better because I had favoritism from my teachers. As always, I love to dance so I joined the dance team in my high school. We performed mostly in front of big crowds. In addition to that, I also modeled with a few companies but never got paid for it. Modeling will never be my actual purpose and destiny in school or life: sometimes, we might end up on the wrong path of our destiny but our internal GPS, the Holy Spirit, reroutes us to the right path by creating situations that are out of our control.

I was a great girl – daddy's little spoiled princess – doing mostly everything my father said until I got the unpredictable news of my father's death. Life had hit in another painful direction I could not comprehend. As we say sometimes, everything happens for a reason and a specific purpose, even though we may not be able to understand the reason or the purpose.

Chapter 2

Death of the Breadwinner (My Father)

How could God take our Father from us so fast knowing he was the only breadwinner? I was so young, innocent, and naïve. I was mad at the world and God at that time. Death really exists. We never accept the fact that we are living in a temporary body and one day we will leave these bodies. I had to face the reality of life and accept the fact that my father was dead due to simple heart failure after being paralyzed. My father did not talk a lot about his childhood but I could tell by the way he treated us, that he wanted all his children to become better versions of himself. My grandparents were immigrants from Nigeria. They kept their family tradition: Yoruba (Nigeria tribe). That is why I practiced the Islam religion from birth until the age of 19. I converted to Christianity when I was born again (of the Spirit, as is written in God's Word).

I was in my first year of college when my father passed away. I can remember, like yesterday, when my father was very sick and was rushed to the emergency room with a heart attack. It was shocking to everyone because we did not see it coming. The reality of my father's death hit me hard. We were going to lose everything with my father being hospitalized. He was a great father, and a good provider even though I never had his presence in the home, and felt fatherless during my childhood.

According to Muslim tradition and culture, a man has the right to marry as many wives as he wants and has to treat them equally, which was, of course, not the case. Before I was born, my father's first wife had died so the second wife became the first one automatically. My older sister witnessed a lot of fights and jealousy between the wives, and I don't know how she survived all those traumas: I could not imagine growing up in such an environment. However, it became even worse after my father passed away. Besides the tradition and cultures, my father wanted his second wife to be happy so there would be no conflicts between her and any of the other wives. He was a great peacemaker so he tried to keep the entire family together. It was an easy task for him, especially since everyone wanted his love and attention: I mean, he had three existing wives and 22 children at that time. He lived 24/7 with his second wife who was very jealous and very evil. Sometimes, she did not want me to see my father. She would say that he was not there even when he would be in the house. Even though I felt like I was born into a dysfunctional family I have learned that my father valued our education and growth like any good father does. He wanted the best of the best for his children. He made sure that we went to the best schools: his main goal was that we excelled and got good grades and degrees because he did not get that opportunity when he was a child. My grandparents did not believe in education, especially for girls but my father changed and broke that cycle by putting us; his daughters, in the best schools in our city. He was very proud when I was the first daughter to graduate from high school with honors. I never forgot the joy on his face to see his younger daughter graduate. I had the opportunity that he never had in his life. He told all his friends and took me to a nice restaurant where we ate and celebrated my achievements. Even though my father was not present in my home he loved me. I was his favorite daughter since birth. The love that my father showed me, in the short time of his life with us has made me into the loving, kind, resilient, patient and strong woman I am today, and I have learned that it is important to give love to others no matter what the circumstances. He was always ready to provide for us.

My father's death was a wake-up call for me to start seeking my own survival on this planet. Imagine everything was given to you on a silver platter: food, schooling fees, clothing and any luxury you could think of. Then you get the news that your breadwinner is dead. What would you do? I had so many questions popping into my mind: How am I going to survive with no allowances to buy everything I want? How are my mother, my siblings, and I going to survive without food? How are our basic needs going to be met? How am I going to afford my tuition fees? The what, where, when, why and how questions did not bring my father back from death, though. I had to grow up and face the dreadful reality that I was not ready, trained, or prepared for what was ahead.

My mother did not have any income at the time. Her small charcoal business was not producing enough income for us to make it through the months. We struggled a lot – not only emotionally, physically, mentally but also spiritually and financially.

For almost three weeks, my father was unconscious. He was fed by way of a nasogastric tube. When I visited him he could not speak. My siblings and I tried to alternate the visits so that every day one of us was there to help. I cried a lot and was depressed most of the time when I left the hospital. I lost my appetite, and I could not explain what his current situation was – to my mother or my siblings, when I got home.

December of 1999, exactly 3 weeks before Christmas, was the last time I saw him. That is why I am not too much into holidays nowadays: It reminds me of when my father took his last breath from this earth. I recall how I knew he would not survive one more day on this earth. I could sense the smell of death in his room. My father was totally paralyzed and lying down in the bed when I visited him. I prayed to God, Jesus Christ, and the Holy Spirit to heal him and give him a second chance. By that time, I had already changed my religion from Islam to Christianity but my father had no knowledge of it. I was afraid to tell him I was no longer a Muslim because that would not go in line with the woman he wanted me to be, and I could not marry someone that would honor his name. The truth is that I was afraid of the persecutions and loss of honor. To think of the dishonor he would face because of me: I would no longer abide by the Muslim religion and practices. I saw how he persecuted my older sister and brother when they confessed their conversion to him. He cut their allowances, stopped paying their school fees, deprived them of food, and kicked them out of the house. It was a traumatizing scene to witness as a teenager. The idea of being completely disowned. I feared all of the backlash, so I pretended to be a Muslim girl until his deathbed. Deep inside I had already given my life to Jesus Christ and was water baptized.

There were good and terrible outcomes for this part of the story of my life. The good news: I was not given to an older man to be a wife to have many children with no purpose, and I did not have to keep practicing the Muslim religion which I was not interested in or attached to spiritually whatsoever. Eventually it was time to face reality and learn how to survive on my own. At that time, I did not have professional learning skills to look for a great job.

Even though I graduated from high school, transitioning as a freshman at the University of Lomé, I had no job experiences or internships with companies. I was challenged however, to look on the bright side of things. I was maturing into adulthood and into the future by making good choices and decisions that would define my next generation. I then had the choice either to break a generational curse or create a generational wealth. It is called – Welcome to a survival mode – another brutal story of my life.

Chapter 3

Ultimate Survival

It did not feel like "home" while growing up because of the tensions and constant fighting among us as children. I felt homeless emotionally, physically and financially before and after my father's death, because my mother and all of us children had to move away from our house. The reason why we had to flee was that, my half-brother threatened to burn us alive with gasoline while we were sleeping. He said that if we planned to stay longer in the house that my father had built for us (my mother and siblings), he would do everything to keep us away from the house. After his threat, my mother told us that we had to leave and go as far away from him as possible.

My mother rented a big moving truck and we left the house with all of our belongings. We moved into a two-bedroom apartment: can you imagine the life of seven people living in two bedrooms, sharing a kitchen and bathroom with other tenants? It was not a pretty situation for me as a young woman and my family. Can you imagine living in fear, becoming fugitives for the sake of survival because of your own family? Our living situation did not get better, but we got some help from my other siblings who were abroad. With their help we were able to move into a townhouse. It was while we were trying to settle in with our new life, that we got hit with the news that my father was hospitalized due to a heart attack. One of the things that contributed to his heart attack, which made him very sad, was that we left without telling him about the situation with my other siblings. With the circumstances surrounding our runaway: the threats we were getting from our half siblings, we did not have any choice. Can you imagine becoming a deserter by choice because you wanted to live and see the sunrise before darkness took you away for good?

There were questions popping in my head. How could I survive after my father's death or pay for my school fees? How was I going to make money at such a young age? It was at that time my mother decided to sell charcoal to help us a little bit. Charcoal was the most efficient fuel that most people in Togo used for cooking because we did not have ovens or gas systems at that time. Sometimes, I would buy wholesale soaps and any other items that I could sell to gain profit to help my family and myself. I walked many miles to sell those soaps and items so that I could get some money, rain or shine. I cried sometimes. I looked up in the sky and asked, "Is there a God in heaven that sees our pains and struggles? Why does God always seem so silent when we go through so many trials in life?" The only answer I got at that moment was: TRUST THE PROCESS. On the other hand, my mother continued to get charcoal from her suppliers – wholesale with no money down. We lived in hope daily, to sell a lot of charcoal before the debtors came for payment. The struggle was no joke back then. I feel so blessed today, even though my goals and dreams are not yet fully accomplished. I am so thankful today that I did not prostitute myself or binge on any drugs as many young girls do when they face hardships such as mine. I never thought about it. It never even crossed my mind because I grew up in a house where I had a strict lifestyle with a dress code and where alcohol was not permissible. With not enough money we managed to survive with what we had at that time. The real truth of how my family and I survived after my father's death was that we had each other's back – that is, my mother and her children.

My father's funeral was arranged very fast. In the Muslim religion, dead bodies are buried quickly. Most women are not allowed to see dead bodies or go to the cemetery for burial ceremonies. To be honest I do not know where my father's body was buried. My mother went through many widow traditions by sitting on the mat for a month with my other stepmothers as well. It was not a happy moment to lose loved ones, especially a breadwinner. My father was a very hard-working man but he did not leave us anything or write a will. My stepmother and half siblings who lived in his big unfinished house, seized everything: his assets, bank accounts and the entire business. We were stripped from every single asset of my father, and sadly, there was nothing we could do. We could not even fight legally for anything. I remembered shortly after my father passed away, I did an inventory of his business that amounted to more than 3 million CFA (Central African currency). Money can buy anything but not in my father's case. He was a millionaire before and after his death but his money could not save his life. I learned many lessons at this time including the fact that money cannot buy us our health or an eternal life. If that were the case my father would still be alive until today. Some people said to me, "Your father was cursed by elders or ancestors." However, I did not believe that. All I knew at that time was that I could not concentrate in my first year of college.

I was very depressed, grieving over my father's death, traumatized and sad every day. I missed a lot of classes. I even had many thoughts about dropping out of college. My situation even got worse when I was hospitalized with an unknown illness. I was paralyzed in bed for three months. My life events were not glitter or gold at all. At that time there was painfulness, sadness, and brokenness. I have become strong and believe the best for me and my family today, because of all I went through. No words can describe the pain I felt when my father died. I could say the pain was like a knife planted in my chest . I was hurt and I needed a lot of healing in order to proceed to the next chapter of my life. I have learned that a loss is loss, as Theresa Caputo (New York Times Best Seller Author) says in her book titled: Good Mourning: Moving through everyday losses with wisdom from the other side: *"Every one of us experiences daily losses, big or small. We can see them coming or they can completely blindside us. They can tear us down or make us stronger. And the more we learn about how to cope with them, the faster we will recover. Until then, it is simply enough to get a little stronger, and a little better, every day. And that is where Spirit and I come in."*

The things that keep me going in life are my faith in God and my resilience to believe big for my future generation, and for myself to leave a legacy. My illness was another chapter of my life story which was very sad and painful – more than my father's death. People said that I was lucky when I survived, but I do not believe in luck – I believe in God's miracles. No one saw it coming: against all odds, I survived it ALL.

Chapter 4

Healed from Unknown Illness

It was shortly after my father's funeral that we moved to the townhouse that my older sister from America helped us to rent. I am still grateful to her for all the sacrifices she had made for the family since our father's death. We tried to focus on a fresh start and put everything surrounding our father's death behind us, but another tragedy was waiting on our doorstep. Just when we thought we could breathe again, I was unexpectedly plunged into a coma, a terrifying experience that would leave me fighting for my life for three long months.

The property owner welcomed us in a friendly manner but later we felt like she was jealous of our lifestyle. Against all odds, we were strong together. On the 2nd of January of 2001, the day after New Year's, I woke up with a fever, nausea, and severe headaches. I remembered we had a big New Year Eve party the night before. I thought I was tired because we ate, danced, and sang a lot. It was supposed to be a small party but it turned out to be big with many friends and some members of my local church. First, my entire body felt cold, then I started throwing up in my bedroom, on the path to the bathroom, and everywhere else. There was no alcohol at the party, plus my family and I did not drink at all at that time. Immediately, my family called a nurse to give me a flu shot. To be honest I had no idea what was inside of that syringe so I resisted and refused to take it. However, I was tackled by my mother and sisters to keep me from moving and could not move when the nurse injected me with the shot. In a minute, after the nurse injected me, I fainted. I drifted away from the hands of everyone. I lost consciousness and was rushed to an emergency room. The pains in my body, hands and toes were unbearable. When I arrived at the hospital, the nurses gave me antibiotics that put me in a more dangerous situation for three months. I ended up in a coma.

When I came out of the coma it was like a resurrection: a long three months fighting between life and death. I was told that I ended up in three different hospitals. Most of the events that happened between those transfers I was not aware of. My family told me that I screamed the whole time saying that something was burning like a fire in my entire body. Of course I could not move my body or do anything for myself, without the assistance of my family. I became dependable on my mother and my sisters. I could feel the sadness in their eyes when they came to visit me while I was in and out of consciousness. Pain was my new normal. Every time I saw the sunshine in the hospital room, I put my hope and trust in God who is my healer, that one day I will be pain free. That's what kept me alive. During my ordeal in the hospital, my mother and siblings kept vigil by my bedside daily.

Despite all the medical exams, no specific cause of the illness was determined. Nurses and doctors were doing everything to keep me alive. I was told that my room even smelled like death. Sometimes nurses were afraid to come to my room to provide care, such as changing bandages and bed sheets. My skin, legs, arms, and face were infected.

I was given antibiotics to kill and stop the spread of the "unknown infection", but amidst the traumas and pains I was still breathing. God kept me alive due to the prayers and fastings of my family and church brothers and sisters. My fingers and toes were numb; they felt like they were falling off. My skin peeled off on the bed sheets. It was painful. My doctor consulted my family to amputate my fingers in order to stop the spreading of the "unknown infection" to my organs.

It was a hard decision especially for my mother and me, but that was the ONLY feasible option. That is why I am alive until today. The surgery was scheduled and was very successful but I was very sad to know that I lost six of my fingernails (4 on my left hand and 2 on my right hand) and some of my toes (all of my right toes were amputated). It is challenging to choose a shoe size that fits all the time, but I get to choose. Life is beautiful. I cried a lot and went without food; sometimes for a whole day because of my lost appetite. I started to recover little by little after the surgery, like getting out of the bed to walk around the hallways of the hospital with the help of my mother.

People always say, "What does not kill, makes you stronger" and I found strength, hope, faith, love, resilience, and courage to keep going and live. Today I am alive because of my faith in God and the financial assistance of my siblings living abroad: my older sister with her husband in the USA and older brother who was living in Belgium. Of course, the hospital stay was expensive. The bill was enormous for the three months that I had stayed there. I have kept most of the receipts with me until today. They are proof of the fact that God took the evil in my life and turned it into goodness for me and my family.

I was told that it was the best private hospital in my city with great doctors. After I got discharged from the hospital, I still had to go through numerous physical therapy and checkups. I was not able to go to college because I was ashamed of people's opinions, and the way they looked at me as if I was cursed. In addition to that, I was not able to write or read because my vision was also affected. Sometimes, I could barely open my eyes. I wanted so badly to live the normal life I used to. Deep down inside I was very sad because I felt that I had become a burden to my family. I was dependent on them for help with simple things like eating, bathing and moving around the house. However, in spite of the physical, mental and emotional challenges, I did not give up. I started to learn to grasp things with my hands and to write again. I wanted to be a normal and independent human being like the one I used to be.

Through the ordeal my family supported me a lot with their prayers. They sometimes even made me laugh with their jokes – especially my mother. I lost many friends, including my boyfriend, who was my highschool sweetheart. He came and broke up with me while I was recovering. It is funny how life can turn upside down, when we trust people to be there for us in our most difficult times but they actually disappoint, betray or let us down. That is why I put my trust in God only, who is the Author, the Perfecter and Finisher of my faith.

I suffered a lot with disappointments, betrayals, traumas, anxieties, and Post Traumatic Stress Disorder (PTSD). That is why self-love and self-care, combined with my faith in God are very essential to me every day. When I was home bound, I became more depressed about my current situation. At that time, I thought about hurting myself and even attempted to commit suicide. In my culture, there is a significant lack of support for individuals facing mental health challenges, and that is truly unfortunate. This gap in understanding and care is really troubling because I personally needed help, and I know so many others could benefit from receiving mental health support from their community, neighbors, and family. In my case, my family was aware of my struggles, so I was never left alone; they ensured someone was always watching over me. Fortunately, I didn't end up in a mental facility or institution, but the truth is, such options aren't even considered in my culture.

I know I wrestled with my mental health both during and after the healing process, and I can't help but wonder how much more manageable that journey could have been in a culture that embraced mental health support as a possibility. A more compassionate and supportive approach would make such a difference in the lives of countless people.

Nevertheless, God Almighty had another plan for my life and my future as Jeremiah 29:11 *For I know the plans I have for you, declares the Lord, plans to prosper you and not to harm you, plans to give you hope and a future.* While I was going through my pity party, my family was planning to get me out of the city in order to move to America for a better living situation and better healthcare. The process of coming to America was not as easy as many people thought. It required a lot of paperwork and financial aid, but with God's favor and blessings on my life I was able to get through it and was granted a student visa in order to move to the United States after three consecutive attempts. I never saw myself living in my home country being incapacitated due to what had happened to me. I wanted to get out as soon as possible after recovering from my illness. Again, I would not accomplish this process without my resilience, and the prayers and support of my family. I am here today alive and sound because of the power of resilience I had in me since birth.

There were so many strange and evil things that happened to me during my childhood – things I did not understand, or grasp until now. One thing I have understood is: *what then shall we say of these things? If God be for us, who can be against us?* (See Romans 8:31). I implore my readers, not to give up on yourself and dreams in life. Remember, your resilience and belief in yourself will take you as far away as you can ever imagine yourself. Reach out to the stars, don't just reach out to them, grab hold of one, grasp it tightly and pull into your heart and soul. Let the sky be your limit. Do not let anyone dictate your future but God and yourself. You are here for a specific reason, do not sell yourself short or settle for less than what you deserve. You are the creator and the designer of your life and future. ALWAYS remember this: Be happy! You will get to your Promised Land, as I did!

Chapter 5

Moving to the Promised Land

Many people think moving to America is like a piece of cake, as the expression goes. Some might assume that all you need to do is to just pack your luggage and buy a plane ticket. It is not anything remotely close to that or the "Coming to America" movie I wished for. Some foreigners might even think that they can come with no visa and be able to see all the 50 states at once. It is certainly not the case. It requires a lot of money, paperwork, dedication, faith, courage, resilience and patience; and of course, a visa.

After my unknown illness I was very tired of everything. I did not want to live anymore. I wanted to vanish and hide from everyone and everything. Isolation was not my only contemplation, death joined it too. It crossed my mind all the time. Yes, I was tired of being looked down on by people in my city whenever I got out of the house. I was labeled a curse and forbidden from the society that I thought would love me for who I was, no matter what. I wanted to isolate myself but it was not easy at all. Living with my physical condition was very depressing.

My family decided to get me out of the city as soon as possible for fear of being hurt by others. The first process was for me to get out and go to the USA for better treatment for my hands, scar tissues, and better physical therapy. As I had mentioned in my previous chapters. I went through numerous physical therapies to regain my ability to walk properly and to write and read again. I thank God for my mother and my siblings' support. I feel like I owe them a lot, especially my mother. I cannot imagine the agony and hurt she was experiencing to see me going through everything that I had been through.

It was a miracle how fast my visa was processed. To get a visa quickly in my country, one has to know someone in the embassy, buy his/her position to get it, or by bribing. Did I have to take the shady path or cut the corners? No! I followed the proper procedures and trusted God for a miracle. Fortunately, I was granted a student visa to move to the USA in December that year, after a couple of attempts. Usually, the process would take a few weeks or months before one can get an interview in person.

The anguish that I felt while going through the process of applying for my visa was unbelievable. The first attempt was for medical purposes so I could get better treatment for my hands' movements, scar tissues and physical therapy. I got denied on the spot with no explanation. A few days later, I left the house with the same documents without telling anyone in my family that I was going back to the embassy. I rented a motorcycle taxi round trip even though my health condition prevented me from using any form of transportation per my doctor recommendation. I just told the motorcycle guy to go slowly, not faster until we got to the embassy. I could recall, according to the stamp in my passport, that it was exactly five days after the first denial. Supposedly, no one is allowed to apply or go back to the embassy, until after a couple of months. I did not care about that rule. I went anyway, and got denied for a second time. It is funny and I laugh about it every time I think about that moment. I was very stubborn and wanted everything to go my way and on my time. Since childhood, I have always had an indomitable spirit. That spirit within me will fight against all odds. I was unique and did the opposite of everything my siblings did. In other words, I was a strong-willed risk taker.

The second denial gave me a clearer insight concerning all the other documents that I would have needed to apply for my visa under a different category. I came home and told my family that we needed to try another route, which was to better my education in the USA. I could then become a potential candidate for an American corporation upon graduation from college. They thought I was very crazy to go back to the embassy by myself, not to mention my physical and emotional state, but I don't take failures lightly.

I was born to shine and would not let anyone or anything dim my light. One night, I had a dream about leaving my country, even before I was granted my visa. Yes, it did come true with my faith in God, prayers and fasting. The third attempt was successful. I was granted a student visa, and my mother was granted a tourist visa so she could help me all through the trip due to my inability to grasp things with my hands since my surgery. In addition to that, my physical, emotional, and mental condition at that time was not stable and I would definitely need help throughout the journey to Denver. Eventually I had to leave by myself because the airfares were too expensive for both me and my mother.

I did not leave my country until mid January of the following year however, because my family needed to figure out everything concerning accommodations and travel preparation. I wish my coming to America was like in the movies or fairytale. However, I was patient enough to go through the process and the hardships that came along with it. I was so excited to leave my country but sad to leave my family and all the joyful memories. I packed all my clothes, shoes, handbags, and the most important legal documents such as passports, birth certificates, high school certificates, and anything that I thought I might have needed in the USA.

I was ready to embark into the unknown. I took the leap of faith and left everything behind as well as my beautiful city, Lomé with its beaches, foods, warm weather, and people. I was afraid to travel by myself, but was trusting that God would guide me through all the way to Denver, Colorado. I did not go through my city's airport to come to the United States of America because my family wanted everything to be done covertly. I traveled to Accra City (Ghana's next neighboring country) with my mother to stay in one of her friend's houses. . It was not an easy decision; I had to say goodbye to my siblings. We cried together a lot. It was very emotional to leave them without knowing if I would be able to see them again. That day was the last time I saw my siblings. They all grew up, got married and had kids and I lost one of my older siblings which will be told later in another very emotional story.

I was ready to leave my city Lomé for good. I was ready to leave my past behind, embrace my situation and leave my future in God's hands.

The Journey Has Begun

My mother and I took a bus at night to the border between my city Lomé and Accra. We did not need any visa to travel to Accra city. All we needed was our valid Togolese passport to cross the border. We traveled three and half hours in a car – almost 105 miles from the border. I could not sleep: I had too much on my mind and some questions I could not answer. I was anxious and panicking. My mother was worried about me, but I gave her the assurance that I would be fine.

I owe my mother a lot. She has been there for me since day one of my illness. It was a joy for her to see me leave to pursue my education, dreams, and better medical treatment. So I arrived at Accra Airport with the help of my mother and her friends. That was not a dream anymore. I boarded the plane late at night. I was on my way to the United States of America to Denver, Colorado. The struggle was real and very emotional. Before I boarded the plane I started crying.I clung to my mother. I wanted to stay and not get on the plane. However, I pulled myself together, wiped my tears, and with my head up, I passed through security to board my plane. I hugged and kissed my mother after we prayed and she said, "This too shall pass, the evil the devil meant for you, God has turned for greater good for your life. Be strong, my daughter." (in Ewe language). Then I hugged her again. I did not want to let go of her, but I had a plane to catch. I left my mother behind the airport glasses and hallways to my boarding gate. I was strong but scared inside because I never flew on an airplane before . I boarded on the KLM (Royal Dutch Airlines). I breathed in and out and reminded myself that I was flying to America "The Promised land". I had the assurance that God was with me all the way. My first stop was in Amsterdam (Europe) at 6am. It was an eight-hour flight from Accra to Amsterdam. This was only a quarter of my journey to the promised land. I thought I was lost on my journey or missed my itinerary. I started asking people questions in French. I was reassured that I was at the right place to fly to my next stop. I had to wait another 4 hours until my next flight heading to Minneapolis, Minnesota (USA). I tried to rest and relax but I was afraid of falling asleep and missing my next flight. I wandered around the airport to find something to eat but nothing really caught my eyes that could fill my appetite. I was hungry physically but the excitement of this adventure filled up my stomach. I just wanted to finish this journey and meet my family in Denver, Colorado. I was tired and hungry. Fortunately, the airplane attendant fed us when I got on the next plane.

I remembered falling on the escalator, trying to get to my next flight connection. It was very embarrassing, but I struggled and got up after that shameful scene. Yes, I am still here and alive. Anyways, I was able to get on the next plane to Minneapolis – my first stop in the "promised land". From that point I was thinking, though tired, in body, mind and spirit: *At least I made it to the United States of America.* Obviously I could read a big sign at the airport saying, "WELCOME TO THE UNITED STATES OF AMERICA". I went through the immigration process checkpoint for security and verification purposes: It was a long line but I made it to the immigration officers. They checked everything: my passport with stamped valid visa, handbag, coat and my three pieces of luggage, full of clothes, paperwork and food. I meant they took everything out from the top to the bottom and threw away anything that would not be acceptable on American soil. Since 9/11 airport security has been very tight and stressful. In my mind I thought "OMG I might end up with nothing" Fortunately, they cleared me through the immigration process and security checkpoint. Then, after answering a few questions about my stay in the USA, they provided me with a little card with my immigration identification number stamped on the back of my Togolese passport. It was my INS number and was proof that I came to the US legally. After that, I headed to the final boarding gate for my final flight to Denver, Colorado to meet my family. It took about an hour to arrive at Denver airport. At that point, I was already exhausted. I was awestruck when I saw how beautiful and huge the airport in Denver was. I had no clue that I had to take a train to get my luggage at the luggage claim area. Once I figured it out (by asking people questions) I was able to shuffle to the luggage claim area and collect all my suitcases.

My family was anxiously looking for me; they thought I was lost or got stuck somewhere along my long trip. Eventually they located me and helped with my luggage and we headed home. On our way to the house, the beauty of Denver city fascinated me which is why I never left. I fell in love with the city and everything about it at first sight. Yes! I made it to the promised land.

Now, let us talk about the culture shock: from people, weather, time zone, values, morals, foods, and language barrier. I encountered a lot of problems but I developed more patience to find solutions in order to build my entire life and make my American dream come true. Do not take me wrong, life in America is not that bad, but there has been hard work involved, sacrifices, resilience, and strength, above all, I developed the courage to keep going everyday despite all the challenges I had to face. In one statement: life in the promised land has not been easy,I had to face giants every single day but I made it work.

Chapter 6

My life in the Promised Land (Culture Shock)

I finally made it to America The home where eagles fly higher, where you can do or be anything you want to if you have the desire in your heart to accomplish them. My life in the promised land has not been as great as most people from the rest of the world think or see in Hollywood movies. It is not a fairytale; it is not the American dream we immigrants think it will be. It is hard work to never give up on yourself, your dreams, and goals to become the person that you want to be. Did the beauty of the promise land with its high skyscrapers, beautiful homes, landscaping, mountains and shopping malls amaze me? Did culture, foods and people shock me? Did I ask myself why people have so much freedom to do whatever they want? Yes, I did at the time, but I am no longer mesmerized as I am now used to this way of life.

I looked back on my journey from Africa to Denver and I could not believe that I finally made it to America. It was a time to face reality and my giants. I thought: *They are nothing compared to the giants in the Bible – like those of Israel of the old days.* Though I was afraid, I had to face them by believing and trusting in God. I thought that if I could make it this far, there would be no mountain too high or valley too deep that I could not conquer.

The next day after my arrival, my older sister helped me to settle down with everything like putting my clothes and other belongings away. I lived with my sister and husband while I attended school on a student visa. Since they were my sponsors, they had to take me to my college so I could report to my director and start classes right away. I remembered this quote, "There is NO rest for the wicked". It was a time to experience life in the promised land. Immediately, I enrolled in the English course so that I could keep my student visa status. That would allow me to work part time on campus after I received my social security number and work permit.

With the help of God I grew strong mentally, physically, emotionally, socially, and financially. First, let me talk about being strong mentally. I was not a good fit mentally as a newcomer in the promised land; however, I saw a lot of negativity in society itself, families' lives, televisions, schools, and on the streets. I asked myself many questions in my little African brain, but I didn't get all my answers right away because I was still in my African mindset and was not trying to grasp everything, nor did I see the positive aspects at that time. My morning routine consisted of waking up, praying or meditating , brushing my teeth, taking a shower, and getting dressed. I had to wear several warm layers of winter clothes.It was the winter season when I got to America and it was bitter cold every morning. I was mesmerized when I saw snow on the ground for the first time, and it was very beautiful to see and feel snowflakes falling on my face and on me. However, even with the beauty of the snow, I am from the tropical side of the world and cold is not my love language even now. Every morning, I helped my sister make breakfast, packed my lunch, then went to my English classes. There was always a rush in the house, every weekday except on weekends. Sometimes I could not keep up with it. I did not have the balance to run back and forth. It was overwhelming and stressful. I thought about what I put myself into all the time. At that time my sister was a hair stylist and owned a hair salon on Colfax Street next to the East High school. It was not far away from downtown Denver – same with my English school.

I also really admire my sister: she is a very strong, mature, wise, and clean woman and a great cook. I learned a lot from her during my stay with her and her family: cooking, cleaning, organizing and balancing her life as a sister, wife, successful business woman and mother. It was not easy but I saw her fulfilling all those duties in a timely manner. I tried to keep up with her but she was too quick for me – handbags, coat, lunchbox and keys picked up all at once. I was trying to adjust physically but my body was not adjusted to America's fast paced life.

I enrolled in English classes so I could improve my speaking, reading and writing. My sister would drop me at school after she dropped off my niece who was in middle school. I eventually figured out the bus system to get back to my sister's salon after class ended. I attended Colorado School of English located in the middle of downtown Denver. I remembered that on my first day I was very shy. I was not able to speak a word. My English teacher wanted us to introduce ourselves to our classmates. I was very soft spoken and nervous because my English was not as good as it is today, especially my speaking, reading and writing. I was very shocked when she asked if we had houses or huts in my country. I laughed a little bit and said, "Of course we have houses, not huts. I lived in a very nice house in the beautiful city of Lomé with nice beaches and nice weather." I did not blame her for such ignorance because to the rest of the world Africa is just a continent full of black people who live in the jungle; chasing animals every day.

I realized very quickly that most Americans do not have any knowledge of Africa and whatsoever. They believe only what is shown in the news about Africa, which is always the bad side like poverty, joblessness, murders, political corruption, and all the other awful things. Every person has a choice to learn or unlearn and believe or not believe what he/she sees or hears floating around on social media. I always say seek knowledge and you will be powerful and greater than you think you are. If we decide not to seek knowledge or wisdom we die. In the Bible, God says, *My people are destroyed because of lack of knowledge* (Hosea 4:6).

I am a fast learner, and I love to learn so it took me about seven months or so to learn American English, because I had learned British English before I decided to move to the states. There was always homework after each class: writing, speaking, reading, research papers, and essays. After class, I took the bus to my sister's hair salon and waited for her until she was finished with her customers. She worked very hard. Sometimes we would get home very late because she would have too many customers and sometimes she would accept walk-ins and last-minute appointments.

As time went by, I started becoming very tired of my routine, so I would just go straight home after school. I was bored, sad, and unhappy. Sometimes I cried a lot, and my emotions were all over the place. I started to miss my mother and other siblings back home. I know that they were happy for me but I could not go back.I wanted to explore the city of Denver more with its beautiful scenery. I wanted to go to the library, museums, visit parks, mountains, shopping malls, and travel to other states, but I did not have a job. I had applied for my social security number and work permit. This process could take 3 to 9 months or even a year after arrival. I was patient enough and remained in a prayerful state. One day, I got my prayers answered; my social security card and work permit arrived in the mail with restrictions to work part time only, while I was still on my F1 student visa. I started looking for jobs immediately so I could help my sister pay my tuition and be able to purchase things for myself. She and her family already had too much on their plates. I helped her around the house when I could. On the weekends, I cleaned, did laundry, and organized things around the house to the best of my ability. That way, after long hours of working, she did not have to do anything else other than cook for everyone. My big sister is Wonder Woman. She can do it all by herself; believe it or not. She got that strength and spirit from our mother and so do I. So I too wanted to be independent financially.

After many attempts of putting in applications, I got a job at this retirement community facility called "Park Place" as a housekeeper for part time. It was not my dream job, but it was a job to start making a steady income. I was proud of myself. It supplied my basic needs. It was a great start to build my resume because I did not have a college degree. I was making little money but I was happy. This changed my routine somewhat as I was now going to school and working. My job description was not easy but I managed to give it my best. It consisted of cleaning eight rooms during my shift. If I was done early, I had to clean the common area including the hallways, activities center, gym, and dining room for the elderly. I was shy, and introverted according to my personality test. I did not make any friends from either school or work and I had my reasons: I did not trust anyone after everything I had gone through in Africa and since I arrived in America. However, I trusted one woman as time passed. I became friends with one white, older woman who was a hairstylist for the elderly. The first time that we spoke, she thought I was like a 13-year-old girl working at that place. She asked me, "Why did your parents let you work here?" I laughed and said, "I am over 20 years old and I can show you my state identification". Until today people have the same impression of me: they say I look 10 years younger than my actual age. Remember the saying, "BLACK DOES NOT CRACK": especially black women. We became friends from day one. She broke down my walls and boundaries and got to know me for who I was. I could be myself around her. She took me to other places and cities outside of Denver for different events.

My social life in the promised land was getting better. I was not bored anymore. We had breakfast, lunch, and dinner together. She invited me several times to her house for family gatherings, holidays, and other special occasions. We became best friends. She supported, directed, and gave me wise advice. When I moved to my first apartment, she bought me furniture and kitchen supplies. I keep in touch with her until this present day. It is very surprising to me that I am not introverted anymore and have become a people person. I was balancing my job and schooling for a year or so and was adjusting to American culture and people. It was not easy but I did it and I am still doing it. I did not like fast food because in my country we do not have them, and my mother cooked every meal fresh for us from breakfast to dinner every day. That is why we have great longevity and a low mortality rate in my country.

After a while I wanted to do something different, a different job. So I transferred to a technical school so I could learn computer applications. I wanted to better myself in every level of my education. My dream was to become the first woman in my family to hold an American degree, and my dream did come true.It took me a long time but I did get that degree. After six months as a housekeeper, I started to dislike my job because my supervisor pulled me aside and spoke to me about some complaints that she had gotten pertaining to me. Some of the residents at the retirement place did not like me as a black woman entering in and cleaning their rooms. "Seriously," I said, "I thought people were over this race card a long time ago, like decades ago." Apparently, they were not over the stereotype and are still not over it today. Racial stereotypes and discrimination in this country are out of control, in my opinion, and it makes me sick to my stomach. I believe there is only one race: the Human Race. I do not like to have conversations about this topic. I have learned from my English classes a long time ago: do not ask about people's weight, income, sexual orientation, religion, race, or political affiliation. Just accept everyone the way they are. I am very sensitive to this topic because I have been a victim of discrimination on various occasions since living in America. My supervisor would not go into details with me but I could read between the lines. I eventually gave them my two-week notice, quit and looked for another job.

****

NEVER SETTLE FOR LESS
THAN WHAT YOU DESERVE!!

I never settle for less, I know I deserve better because I am beautiful, wonderfully made by God, brilliant, strong, smart, and a quick learner. I told my sister that I quit my job and that I was going to move out. I wanted to look for my own apartment and a better job and schooling. She was stunned at the idea but I did it anyway. It became a family talk but she eventually forgave me. This is what families do: we forgive, love each other, and move on.

Some people might think it was irresponsible on my part, or I did not appreciate what she did for me, or maybe I had lost my mind. Contrary to those thoughts, I appreciated everything she did for our family and me since our father's death. However, I believed that it was time for me to fly higher. I needed to be an independent and mature woman, so I took the leap of faith. That was my intention and I am exactly at the point in my life that I have always dreamed of at this moment and time. I called it boldness. Did I make some mistakes or poor decisions later on when I moved out? Yes, I did, but I was able to learn from them and grew more mature and wiser. When I moved out from my sister's house, I did not have anything, including money. I only had my suitcase that I brought from Africa with my clothes and important documents. I became homeless by choice. I took a bus and went to a women's shelter close to downtown Denver to get some help first. I stayed there for three months on probation while looking for a job and low-income housing. I had to follow house rules and be in the shelter before 9pm. If I got there after 9 pm the door of the building would be locked. It was a curfew put in place because there were so many abused women who were victims of domestic violence, fearing for their lives, or women getting hurt by loved ones. I even became friends with a few of them but we lost contact after I left the shelter. I knew about the shelter after doing research because to sharpen my mind – I woke up within a year in the promised land. I started to see opportunities in every corner, and within three months at the shelter, I learned and explored Denver city extensively.

I was assigned a case manager to help me find my first apartment and look for a new job. Eventually, I landed a new job as a part time sales associate and cashier at Mervyns. Then I moved into my first apartment. I later transferred to technical school to study data entry and microcomputer applications. I was happy to complete it within a year and get my diploma in information systems and computer applications. I learned all about computer operations including:Microsoft, Excel, PowerPoint, and emails. I also made a few friends, and soon this little African girl, wearing only African clothes, became an extrovert. My classmates used to tease me a lot, especially one in particular: a white European boy. Later on, he admitted that he had a crush on me. That is another exciting, and juicy story. I applaud myself for my bravery. What a wonderful transition! We were all international students longing for a better life and pursuing the American dream. Some of them keep in contact with me until this present day and some have moved to other states or back to their home countries in Europe, Africa, and Asia.

After I graduated from that technical school, I wanted to further my education. I wanted to attend another four years of college to get my bachelor's degree in business administration and a concentration in marketing. I was ambitious and hungry for accomplishments and achievements, and I wanted to soar higher than I could have ever imagined. I knew the spirit of the promised land was taking me over when I became more positive and started seeing opportunities in every corner. I was rising from ashes to glory. I was not that little girl anymore but I was maturing into a beautiful, mature, sexy, strong, resilient and independent woman. God has really turned all my ashes from Togo to glory in the promised land . From setbacks to comebacks. My mess into a powerful message. My tests into a powerful testimony. I am rising from ashes to glory: I overcame everything that meant to destroy me physically, mentally, emotionally, spiritually and financially.

Chapter 7

Rising from
Ashes to Glory

We all know that eagles don't stay on the ground, they soar as far as they can to reach great heights and without loss of altitude. I have had this eagle spirit since birth and I have no excuses to change for anyone. This chapter of my life is so exciting and inspiring because I became the independent and strong woman I have always envisioned in my mind. I was ambitious and wanted more achievements. There were a few bumps on the way to accomplishing my dream, but my dream came true eventually. I was happy that I got my first apartment not far away from Cherry Creek Mall for $500 with utilities included. I wish I could pay that price these days. Rental prices in Denver have tripled and quadrupled in the last 10 years. The apartment was small but I loved it. It gave me a sense of independence, freedom, peace, security, and safety to focus on work, schooling, my dreams, goals, and deepest aspirations. Like I said earlier, I wanted to pursue a bachelor degree in business administration, which would take four years but it turned out to be more than that for me. I transferred all my credits from all my previous schools to a new college called Teikyo Loretto Heights University (private college) in Federal Heights. After they evaluated all my credits, and my transcripts from my home country, I was told I would get my bachelor's degree in less than 4 years. I was so excited; however, it took me more than four years. I had to be a full-time student in order to keep my student status and with all that school was very challenging. As an international student, I had to pay from my own pocket. International students are not qualified for federal loans unless they become permanent residents or green card holders, and that's the difficult part. It was very strenuous to pay tuition fees, but I managed with my income, scholarship awards and tuition reimbursement from the better full time job that I got.

I kept my job as sales associate at Mervyns for one year or so while going to college until the company had a closure. I received a severance package. All thanks to Jesus! It was not enough but it helped me to survive.

A few weeks later, I got a better job as a customer service representative, which came with a full benefits package: medical, dental, vision, 401k, tuition reimbursement. It was a great international company; I took their inbound and outbound calls in English and French: where customers transferred and received money or paid their bill as well. Being bilingual, I was paid more – a shift differential. I chose that shift because that was better for my classes. I loved my job even though it was challenging. It enabled me to improve my English while taking phone calls with customers. I was climbing the corporate ladder. I could not settle for less than what I deserve. I wanted to better myself spiritually, physically, mentally, emotionally, socially and financially. I had a great balance between full time school and work. I was tired of taking a bus everyday between school, doing my errands, and work. I always kept Sundays off to be in church to worship and thank God for His goodness and faithfulness in my life. What He has done for me no man can do for me.

I decided to buy a car even though I had no driving experience whatsoever. I went to the Department of Motor Vehicles (DMV) to get a learners permit. I passed the written test but I failed the actual driving test miserably on the road. It was not a pretty scene. The instructor told me I would never drive a car on the road: I was a dangerous driver and would be a threat to others on the road. That was his perspective of me at that time. I never accept people's perspectives of me because they are not my God, Creator, or dictator of my future. To be honest, I was afraid of the road rage, highways, and the many drunk drivers on the road. I had to fight to conquer my fears and giants.

Finally, I passed my driving test after multiple attempts and I got my driver's license. I was excited to buy a car that I could afford, to run my busy life. I contacted my case manager and she led me to some dealers who sold used, old cars. Yes, I got my first car; it was an old four door Subaru, which got me from point A to point B, even though I had a lot of panic and anxiety attacks behind the wheels. I also got into a few accidents for a couple of years. I got tickets from the police but I did not go to jail for hitting someone else's car. My driving improved overtime from running back and forth between classes, work, and my personal life. I am very proud of my driving at this point. I have become a professional and safe driver on the road now. A few of my friends say that I drive like a man, but I don't know if that is a compliment or an observation.. I can now drive myself to the mountains within one to two hours without panicking or having an anxiety or panic attack like I used to. If I had listened to that instructor and not faced my fears, I would not be driving in America right now.

Remember, fear is the number one obstacle that stops people from achieving their goals in life. It does not matter how talented they are. I want you to consider this acronym for the rest of your life – the true definition of fear. F.E.A.R is made up of **False Evidence Which Appears Real.** It describes how our minds can weave together false tales of how situations will turn out. Knowing our fears and facing them will set us free. My point here is DO NOT accept people's perspectives of you. You can listen to their advice and say "thank you," but you have a choice to make suitable decisions for you and the future generations. No one knows how to walk in your shoes unless they walk a mile with you. My family does not have a clue about what I went through until now. I am the only one who has expanded my wings and fly to higher heights – heights I thought were unreachable. The sky was my limit. At that time I had only God with me. God is my firm foundation and Provider. Every day when I wake up and see the sun come up and then go down, I give Him praise.

I am no longer the little girl who was a fugitive from her own hometown; who suffered mentally and emotionally from her father's death; who also was tormented with brokenheartedness and survived an unknown illness. She had courage to leave her pains behind and come to America and has grown a lot since then. I am not the girl of my present either, because I have so much further to go. I am the strong woman of my future, with all my past mistakes written on my sleeve as badges of encouragement – a reminder of where I have come from, and motivation for where I am going.

Life in America with its ups and downs made me want to give up at times, but I never took failures lightly. Each failure was another stepping stone to get me to the next level to reach the horizon of my success. I laughed at problems because they were signs telling me that my breakthroughs were around the corner. If I was able to weather all the challenges coming from Africa to America, anyone reading my story can overcome their own struggles. I conquered everything that meant to destroy me. I never stopped in spite of the struggles I encountered through college, especially financially. The tuition fees were becoming very expensive: I would use my rent and food money to get through some semesters. Sometimes, I would take off one or two semesters to reset and get back to classes. After a while the college changed their policies for all international students. We were told that we had to pay up front before classes started. Otherwise, we could not take classes or they would terminate our visa on the spot. I then applied for reimbursement from my full-time job. I tried to make a payment arrangement every month but it was difficult. I could not make the payments because I had other bills to pay as well. I could not keep up with my bills. I even tried to get a roommate to share the rent with me but that was not for me. It started to affect my focus on school, goals, and my peace of mind. Worst of all I got the unpredictable news in my mail that my visa was terminated and I had 90 days to reapply or transfer to another university. I could not afford this inconvenience. Of course, I panicked but, as always, I focused on the solutions instead of the problems. Everything went well: I got my visa back within 90 days, transferred to Colorado Technical University (CTU), where I finally got my bachelor's degree in Business Administration with a concentration major in marketing.

I accomplished my dream to become the first woman in my family to hold an American degree against all odds. You cannot imagine the joy I felt when I completed the last semester at CTU without any student loan balance. I was lucky though, I was a blessed daughter and child of the Most High God. I have a Provider who never lets me down. My student account balance was less than $5000 and I paid it all off after graduation. The journey to my dream was 8 years long: including taking breaks from classes, heartbreaks, dropouts due to financial reasons, and visa termination issues. I could have given up but it was resilience that kept pushing me until I got my bachelor's degree.

I am glad I am not where I used to be. The saying goes, "Strong people are not born, they are made by the storms they walk through." (Soulful.Quotes). I have walked through many storms in the promised land but I never let them knock me down to the curb. I walked straight through them, facing them head on, and came out stronger than ever. Those storms strengthened me and led me to all my breakthroughs. The thing about strong people is that they do not need you, they choose you. And if you ever take them for granted, they will be content without you. That will be your loss..

The joy of the Lord is my strength; God is my strong tower and fortress in times of distress. The devil is a liar. My confidence is in God, not in the things of this world. As a matter of fact, I am living today to declare the works of God and His kindness and goodness in my life. As long as I have breath in my lungs, I will become everything God says about me. Maya Angelou said "Life is not measured by the number of breaths we take, but by the moments that take our breath away." Those moments that took my breath away were when I looked up and said, "I know it is You God; no one else can do this for me so well." Those moments are unforgettable; they will stick with me for the rest of my life. I have to live to tell my story to my children and grandchildren. As Daniell Koepke quotes *"You don't have to solve your whole life overnight.*

And you do not have to feel ashamed for being where you are. All you have to focus on is one small thing you can do today, to get closer to where you want to be. Slowly and lightly, one-step at a time. You can get there." Do not give up yet. The sun is still shining everyday, even on snowy or rainy days. Get out and live your life to the fullest and do not get stuck in any situation that will rob your peace of mind, joy and self-esteem.

Chapter 8

Getting Out From Abusive Relationship

Relationships are complex, tricky, and hard because it is about two imperfect people trying to work together to make something loving, beautiful, and perfect. Relationships are supposed to feel great with the right person, but mine in this chapter turned out to be abusive, and dangerous – a dark story of my life. Everything happened so fast it seemed like yesterday. 2014 was the best year I could ever have imagined. I had just finished my bachelor's degree and wanted to get a master's degree but I did not get a chance to continue because I felt like I needed a break from schooling to focus on accomplishing other things like: settling down, becoming an entrepreneur, meeting my man, getting married, and having my own family in my dream home. I was a happy woman who could see all her dreams come true and everything coming together. I was already engaged to the most handsome, intelligent, brilliant and stable man. It was exciting to be the first woman in my family to hold an American college degree. I felt accomplished that year after struggling through many adversities to get my degree. I was able to enroll in Colorado Technical University while holding two jobs. Thanks to the tuition reimbursement program that my new full time job offered at that time. The company granted me $7500 every year until I finished my courses. It was a great relief to me because I could not make it on my own. While I was in school, my social life was not great: there was no dating or any potential boyfriend. Most of my girlfriends thought that I had higher standards or was not trying to date anyone. They might have had a point then. Why should I date if I did not see any purpose along with it? I prefer to be alone instead of dating someone and become miserable. Besides, no one wants a miserable lifetime partner or to have a relationship where he/she has to prove himself/herself to the other person.

The truth is, I wanted to become stable on every level before I invited someone into my life. I believe that no one can love me the way God loves me. I had many things that I needed to figure out in my life: spiritual, physical, emotional, mentally, financial, health, and career wise. During springtime I had lunch with one of my girlfriends who told me that if I did not take any steps, I would not meet any potential man, or I might end up being alone my entire life. That was a hard truth which scared me. I imagined myself without a potential or future partner, so I took her advice and I went to a dating app to meet new people. I could not have imagined that after so many breakups and heartaches I would decide to date again. It was convenient for me since I was always busy with work and school. It was also risky. However, I created an account on "Match.com" around May of 2014. After a few months with some encounters and messages back and forth with several men, I gave up. I felt like it was a waste of my time and energy so I decided to close my account in July 2014. That is when I got a message from this handsome man who seemed to be interested in me in every level of my life. He was very nice to me and we connected quickly. I loved his mindset, the way he looked at things, and his values. It was not too long after that we exchanged numbers and started chatting off the dating app.

In August of 2014, we went on our first date at Chili's. I really liked him in person. He was very handsome and charming. I fell for his charm, not knowing that a wolf could dress as a sheep. He was everything I or any woman could dream of in a man. He worked hard at that time in the construction business and traveled often between Denver and some other states. He asked me if I was okay with a long distance relationship as he traveled a lot for his job. I said yes, because I was in the last semester of my school year. We talked a lot about many things and laughed a lot. He made me smile every day. Around September of 2014, he asked me to move in with him in his four-bedroom house in Denver, but I said no and told him we were not married yet. He respected my decision and we continued dating. Sometimes he would surprise me with love notes and flowers at my apartment. I was so happy to see him and be with him. It was a safe place for me when I was with him. He knew at that time that I was very vulnerable as I told him about my situation and struggles in the states. He said that I should not worry about it, and that he would help me out after I graduated from college.

Things started getting serious around October when he started talking about our future together. Once he showed me photos of his family ring, through text messages that he would give to me when he saw me the next time. We both were so in love but, inside, I was a very naïve, innocent little African girl who was blinded by love, and at the time, I could not see his true colors. I did not know that he could change like a chameleon and become so manipulative and abusive later on.

During the fall, everything changed to another level. He started talking about love, faith, family, and children. My dreams to settle down were becoming true, so I believed everything he said or told me, and I prayed and fasted for seven days to search and seek for God's will in the relationship.

In November of 2014, I will never forget that date. We went to a Broncos game in a bar in Northeast Denver. After the game, we went home and he got on his knees, asked me to marry him and I said yes. He said that I was strong, beautiful, and a great woman. I was the only woman who accepted him for who he was at that time. We both were so happy and in love. Shortly after the engagement, in December of 2014, I finished all my classes. I was so happy. Everything went so fast within six months. I was ready to graduate in 2015, get married and start having children. It was like all my dreams were becoming a reality. However, this reality turned into a nightmare when in January 2015, I discovered the unbelievable truth on social media. After the holidays, he became so distant from me. He was not returning my phone calls or text messages. He ghosted me after I was wearing his engagement ring on my finger. I trusted him and I was just so worried about him.

One day, I went on his social media account to reach him. Instead of reaching him I discovered that he had another profile of another woman's picture with him together. I was not spying on him at all but the profile came up by coincidence. Today, I could say it was not a coincidence, it was a clear picture of what I call, "Man's rejection is God's protection.

Needless to say, I was shocked and heartbroken. He was living with another woman who was pregnant with his daughter without my knowledge, while I was in Denver being his fianceé all that time. Of course I confronted him and he shut me down. He lied to me and told me that he did not know the woman was expecting his baby. I went to his house, and I knocked and knocked but he would not open the door. I was left heartbroken and cried for almost three months. Even though I could not believe the betrayal I still loved him and hoped that things would work out between us. We could not resolve anything; we just kept arguing back and forth. In March 2015, I got a peaceful message from him, trying to explain the situation. He told me that he wanted to be with me, not the baby's mama. He claimed that it was an unexpected pregnancy and situation. Again, I believed him in spite of what I went through with him emotionally. I waited for my fiancé to come see me in person but he never came to see me. I even invited him to my graduation ceremony with his brother in June 2015. He made excuses not to be there. I was alone with my three friends at my graduation. My family could not make it as well. I was so sad on my graduation day, the day that was supposed to be such a joyous, memorable occasion for that long awaited accomplishment. Later on that week, one of my best friend's mothers surprised me with a graduation party which made me feel a lot better.

It seemed like a whole year had passed by. I had an engagement ring but NO marriage. Later on that year he popped up surprisingly at my apartment. We spoke and he told me everything would be fine as I told him my dilemma about my living and financial situation at that time, and I was not sure what to do. He told me not to worry and to move out from my place because it was not a safe neighborhood. After I moved out, he came to visit me at my new place, took me to the mountains to gamble, and got my mind away from our past arguments. We had fun, ate, drank and gambled, and the rest was a juicy story when we went back to my place. We made love so passionately. Then I became enchanted under his spell again. He gave me specific instructions for the New Year 2016. I had to follow those instructions in order to establish our future together, especially financially. We could get ahead quicker and save a lot of money for marriage and our future family. Unbelievably, I did comply with everything he asked of me. I was like a submissive sex slave to him and he preyed on me so easily.

The year of 2016 was a dark year for me. He gave me an account number from Wells Fargo bank, and half of the money that I made by working two jobs had to go to that account, which was in his name. If I missed a transfer of money, he threatened to beat my ass or call immigration officers at my doorsteps. I was so scared, I just did whatever he asked me. He would give me the silent treatment for weeks or even months until I did what he required of me. I was so sad and I cried a lot in silence. He destroyed me emotionally and mentally. This is the reason why I detest silent treatment from people, especially men. It reminds me of him and the punishment I went through. I am still healing from those emotional wounds and traumas. It will take time, but eventually I will heal completely, because God is my Healer. Sometimes, I would transfer all my savings that I made from my two regular full time jobs to his account, just to stop him from threatening me, or to make him happy. I started to lose my self-esteem, my faith in God, and my values. I thought about hurting myself or attempting suicide. I did not know who I could share my dilemma with. I was living a dark secret and a double life trying to please him and God, from the beginning of 2016 to the end of the year. I was hurting in silence. I felt like I was being eaten from inside out by worms – I had allowed them to enter my being and crawl over my walls and cross my boundaries. Even though I was living in darkness, the little light left in me was still shining. As the Bible says in *Matthew 5:14* "You are the light of the world. A city built on a hill cannot be hidden."

In spite of these situations, I felt the presence, peace, joy, love and protection of God around me every single day. The truth is I was afraid to get out, or maybe dreaming that something magical would happen to make him change his mindset or attitude toward me.

I was still hoping to get married to my fiancé in summer of 2017. He told me that the money transfers I made in 2016 were not enough for us to get a stable, secure and luxurious life. He wanted us to have a great luxurious life, by preying on my innocent and quiet persona. He told me that he would destroy my life if I ever told anyone, especially the law enforcement. The thing that scared me most, however, was when he said that he would beat me to death or showing up on my doorsteps if I did not comply to his demands and expectations. I did not know what to do. I was angry and felt used again. One morning, on an icy, snowy day after we argued over the abusive situations, I drove my car so fast in order to take my life. I did not think I was worthy or of value. My car flipped on the icy road. I was even in shock that I came out alive that day. I ended up in the emergency room. I was taken to two different hospitals, bleeding and bruised inside with no family or friends. I cried a lot, the whole time at the hospital. The only person I could think of was him, but he was not in town that day. I called my pastor who came to help and get me home safe after I was treated for internal bleeding and bruises. My car was a total loss. The insurance could not cover anything. When I asked him to help me to get a new car, he refused and threatened me more. He said that I was lazy and dumb not to listen to anything he told me to do. I told him that I could not do or be what he expected of me anymore by acting like his sex slave or servant, I was done with it for good after the accident.

I did the unthinkable thing, which was to borrow some money from my retirement plan savings (401k). I went ahead to buy a new affordable car in cash. When I told him he made funny jokes about me. He said that I was a very poor and dumb girl since the first day he met me. I cried incessantly till I was weak and debilitated. I regained my strength only when I was completely free from his manipulations and stopped being his sex slave and being the submissive woman by the end of 2017. Can you imagine living in darkness, hurting in silence for almost 2 years? The last time I saw him in person was in March of 2018, around his birthday. We went to an African club where we talked, had a few drinks and he apologized for everything he put me through emotionally, physically, financially and spiritually. He said, "We could be friends but we could never get married because time had passed and I had missed my blessings or window of opportunities." That is the traits of narcissist people. They take and not give back. They make it seem like something is wrong with you, not them. They play the victim mentality game with your emotions and feelings. They do not care about anyone but themselves.

I regained self-consciousness and realized that I was a victim of a controlling, abusive, manipulative, and narcissistic being, and with God's help I got a mighty deliverance out of that nightmare and from under that spell. Praise be to God! I moved on, but with a high degree of emotional pain. I had a lot of healing to go through and I took it one day at a time. I healed myself by reading books on mental health and meditation. I had a lot of anxiety, panic attacks and nightmares but I survived because I am a survivor!

****

Overall, he wasted my time and energy and preyed on me because he knew about my situation in the states. He used my vulnerability against me. He took advantage of me as much as he could and I allowed him to treat me that way. Do I still love him as a human being? Yes, I do, in a cordial and friendly way. I am Sweet Tawa. That is who I am and unfortunately I allowed people to take advantage of my kindness with no boundaries. Now I know better than that. I set boundaries and if you don't respect them I disappear in silence and love you from a distance. I choose distance over disrespect. Maybe, it was all my fault. I should have been stronger for myself and stand on my values. I was weak and fell in love with his charming persona. Sometimes, I feel hate for myself because I let him treat me so badly. I was like a marionette, or maybe I was being brainwashed by him. I am still dealing with some of those nightmares and traumas. It is very hard for me to trust anyone at this moment. I get so scared that people will hurt me, especially men. Though I know there are still good people and good men out there, I am afraid to open up and let my guard down to get hurt again. I don't want anyone to play with my emotions and feelings anymore. I believe emotional wounds take time to heal so I have tried not to rush the process. I am not giving up on love so do not give up either. I want a family structure: husband and wife, father and mother figure, with my kids all living under the same roof. I never experienced that when I was child. I allowed him to take advantage of me, to drag me and turn me into something I did not want to be at all. However, I was wise to see all the red flags, though late, and break free as soon as I could, and escaped the torture. I refused to be the obedient and submissive woman he wanted me to be, letting the relationship fade away. That was not even a relationship: it was a damaged control-ship. I am still dating because I believe I am beautiful and worthy of love and the quality and high value man who is going to swipe my feet off the floor: a real man who will see my real worth sooner or later.

That chapter of my life has taught me a lot about people and how untrustworthy they can be. However, I know that there is still good and humanity in some people. You just need a spirit of discernment and a woman's intuition, or I will say, Holy Spirit guidance, to know and trust the right people. It is okay to trust certain people but you need to build boundaries around yourself because this is an important part of establishing your identity and maintaining your mental health and well-being. Make sure people know your boundaries and respect them. When they don't respect those boundaries then you will know who to choose to be in your inner circle. Choose wisely, protect your boundaries, and build self respect. The key takeaway: Every woman should learn how to walk away from an abusive relationship. She should know her self worth and know that she deserves a man who can treat her like a REAL QUEEN. Love is kind, patient, not easily provoked, not selfish, long-suffering, and not hurtful. You should feel a sense of euphoria in your innermost being when the time is right and you are with the right man. When you feel sad or unhappy in any relationship, that is a sure and clear sign that you need to check out and run as far away as you can before it becomes toxic or depressing. Don't wait too long for red flags to turn yellow or green, because red flags are red flags, trust me on this. You have greatness inside of you and a purpose on earth, do not let anyone or any man take you for granted. You deserve respect, appreciation and love like the TRUE QUEEN you are. Find people who will match your energy instead of changing your energy to please theirs. If I could find my purpose in the middle of the pandemic, so can you. Don't give up yet. There are plenty of fish still in the sea, and some high value MEN still on the earth, looking for high value WOMEN like me and you.

Chapter 9

Turning a Pandemic into Purpose

Is this another hoax or fake news? Was it really a pandemic springing in China, or just another conspiracy story to get rid of the world population? I had no clue that any virus had started in Wuhan, China and traveled to the United States of America. I do not trust the news. I am a firm believer that we should not rely on Television news to define the course of our lives, dreams, and goals in life, but it happened: the pandemic shut down the entire world in an unexpected way. It was like the earth needed a good rest from humanity. I mean, the earth was tired of us making so much collateral damage to the elements that contribute to its survival. The pandemic gave me a sense of discovering my purpose – to know who I was, why I was here, and where I was heading. There were so many questions that hit my mind left and right: How could a tiny virus possibly shut down the entire world in such a way? Why were we not prepared to face that tragedy the way we face natural disasters? What if we were the virus attacking each other and the COVID-19 virus was immunity to help regain our sense of belonging? Why are we always in the rush without slowing down to admire creation around us – breathing the air or even smelling the roses? It is our duty to take a moment to live, love and eat our meals with loved ones and include these in our daily routine. It was like in a dream where I saw everyone wearing masks and walking like zombies. I remembered when 2020 hit I was so happy to see another year full of blessings. In the first month, God blessed me with a new car. Though my credit score was low, I was approved instantly at the car dealer, with low monthly payment and zero down payments. The virus was surprising to me because I had withdrawn myself from all news and most social media platforms such as Instagram, Facebook and Snapchat for a little while. I did that on purpose in order to focus on my goals and myself. I needed a break from all social media to reset for 2020. By mid March, things started getting real. I heard that people were closing their businesses and asking their employees to work from home, and states started to mandate quarantine and social distance. My company provided us with a letter to show to the police in case we were stopped on our way to work. We were considered essential workers. At that time, I was working as a customer service representative in a small call center, but I really did not enjoy working there, it was just another job that paid bills and was for my survival. It was a Technical Company which provided exams for individuals to improve their skills and get licensed in various states. I was thinking that the pandemic was a joke or hoax to scare or reduce the world population. I was still in denial even when I saw most places such as gyms, restaurants, libraries, and movies that I love to go close their doors in my face. I described quarantine as a break for the whole of humanity so we could come to our senses and focus on what was important: to cherish our well-being, families, and friends.

Being indoors for three months and working from home was very boring. I started to discover what I was missing for so many years, my real purpose on this earth. Many questions popped in my mind but three questions stuck out most:

1. Who am I?
2. Why am I here?
3. Where am I going?

My boredom made me create an account on the TikTok app to learn a few dance moves and entertain myself after I finished working at 5pm. Unless I had to get something I needed at my local grocery store, I stayed inside: most groceries were opened at that point. I am so thankful for essential workers until today. They have risked their lives and families to be on the frontline to provide services and care for others, especially nurses and doctors. The truth that no one wanted to accept until now is that the pandemic was really a shutdown of the whole of humanity and a wake up call for us. It either made you crazy or looked for the meaning of life again. It was a wakeup call for us to appreciate our lives instead of complaining about life, or what we don't have. The pandemic exposed a lot about us including our weaknesses and strengths. The quarantine was hard on many of us. We were not accustomed to being home 24 hours a day, seven days a week. In other words, the pandemic either brought our humanity back or made it worse. Families were either coming together or becoming separated. We were used to our routine life: not spending quality time with our loved ones. We rushed through the door with food in our mouths behind the wheels in traffic, when we could have spent precious time with our families and taken time out for ourselves. Some people might say I need to secure my job to pay my bills or feed my family. I called it "modern slavery", which is another controversial topic I do not want to deliberate on here (I may be biased because nine-five jobs were never my strongest suit). That is why I am here to share my story as an inspiration to others. If I could find my purpose on this earth after four decades of living, so can you or anyone for that matter. Look deep inside of you, there is a dormant skill or talent you have never struck or developed. Once you find that talent or passion you are looking for, you will find your purpose. By now, you might be asking where I find my strength. I find it in God through Bible scriptures, meditation, practicing self-love and self-care, and my faith in God. To put it in one simple conclusion, the pandemic was my turning point to find my purpose and to become the best version of myself. I will not change for anything in the world. I love this version of me and the woman I have become.

Chapter 10

Becoming the Best Version of Myself

"If you don't like the road you are walking, start paving another one"-Dolly Parton.

We do not grow when things are easy; we grow when we face challenges. The pandemic happened so fast that I felt as if COVID-19 was an earth immune system for some of us. Personally, the pandemic made me find my purpose in life, my passion for writing, and a better career path. By the end of January 2021, I got fired from my job. I knew it was not serving or helping me to find my real purpose in life anyway. As Job said in Job 3:25 *For the thing I feared has come upon me and what I dreaded has happened to me.* To be honest I never regret getting fired from my customer service job because I saw my demotion as a doorway to my promotion. I have found a real purpose: to be a writer bringing my story to life – an overcomer – overcoming all my struggles in life. I am so grateful for the negative circumstances of my life, because they have strengthened me and helped me to grow spiritually, physically, emotionally, socially and financially. Gratitude is an attitude that has been developing in me every single day. I am so thankful everyday for true friends, family, and for my life. During the pandemic, I spent most of my time at home, because I couldn't go anywhere or do anything except to feed myself. I tried to listen to my body, mind, soul and spirit more, so I could reconnect to my unique well-being again. In the midst of losing my full time job, I did not lose hope because God has always been my provider. I never sat down drowning in self-pity because of my problems; my faith is so strong, nothing can shake it. My faith pillar stands in one of my favorite verses in the Bible, found in Romans 8:28 *And we know that in all things God works for the good of those who love Him, who have been called according to his purpose.* The Bible says, Faith with no work is dead. I believe in the Word of God so I started to look for another way to make an income while applying for housing and utilities assistance from different sources. After two weeks miracles began to happen left and right. I got a part time job as a sales associate at Marshalls, and got approved for rental assistance from an emergency relief fund. That part time job was a doorway to my breakthrough as a writer. That was when I met May Beth (Author) who introduced me to my publisher, Dr. Denise Nicholson. A less than 15-minute conversation turned my whole life upside down. Looking at the timeline from COVID 19, losing my full time job, and meeting her was a clear sign of divine encounter to discover my real purpose in life.

Bloom where you are planted. Every seed you sow on this Earth is either bad or good, and trust me, you will get your harvest. In addition to my part time job, I received COVID-19 relief funds from my apartment complex which proves to me even more that everything happens for a reason. My job underpaid, undervalued and disrespected me. However, I never took the step to call it quits. God created a situation which allowed me to get fired so that I could surrender all to Him and trust Him instead of relying on jobs or people as a source of provision. Not only had that situation opened many doors for me, but it also gave me the opportunity to discover my potential and skills in every aspect of my life. After a few weeks I got my stimulus check and my last check from my former employer. It was as if I was hitting a lottery jackpot in less than 90 days. Losing the job made it seem like I was holding onto something that was not beneficial to me physically, spiritually, emotionally, nor financially. It was like I hit the rock bottom and sprung to the top of the water, and was able to swim without any fears. After I was fired from my unwanted job I saw many open doors for me on all levels. I was able to join the writing incubator challenge to accomplish my dream as a published author. Being an author was a dream which I had in my heart since I was 12 years old. The pandemic might have been a fallout for some people. However, for me it was an opportunity to discover my potential and skills, focus on my purpose, and turn it into the best version of myself. I am so thankful for the woman I have become so far. I may not have everything that I have dreamed of yet, but I am not where I used to be. I have more self-awareness of who I am and who I have around me. I am not concerned about money or material things because nothing in this world or anyone's possessions impresses me anymore. You have to have Jesus Christ as your Savior, Life Insurance, and Alarm System at all times. Some people might say that Jesus is a myth or some old-fashioned Christian religion that keeps people in bondage. That is not the truth. God gave us free will. If we choose life, we are blessed. If we choose death, we are cursed. We each have a choice to make – decisions that will either harm or build us for eternity. I have a firm conviction that nothing can separate me from God and the love I have for Him because He loved and knew me before I was born. In the Bible Jeremiah, 1:5 says. *Before I formed you in your mother's womb I knew you; before you were born I sanctified you and I ordained you a prophet to the nations.* As a matter of fact, this world is the devil's playground so there is nothing in the world that can satisfy my desires and aspirations apart from the Saviour Himself. There is nothing this world can offer me that can quench my thirst for God, because His goodness, kindness, compassion, and love for me surpasses everything that this world has to offer me, including riches and wealth. I do not have words to describe what God has done for my family and me since we have decided to make a new covenant with Him through the blood of his only Begotten Son. I am perfectly loved by God because the Bible says so. He always provides for me beyond my wildest imagination. Every problem or setback I have encountered has turned into solutions and comebacks. For this reason, I want to publicly thank God for the things He has done and is doing for me privately. Life is not always promised but with God, I can stand against any mountain and turn it into a straight path leading to my destiny.

I make a decision every day to be an exceptionally valuable woman so nothing and no one impresses me. I am not the shy African girl anymore, nor am I afraid to speak my mind or be the voice of those who do not have a voice for themselves. I empower myself on every level: spiritually, physically, emotionally, mentally, socially, and financially. This is what I call "SUPERIOR WEALTH". Know who you really are in your sphere. At some point, you have to be in the driver seat of your life because if you are not, life will drive you crazy. This is what I call self-actualization. Be that pen to write your destiny, goals and aspirations. The world needs what you have to offer. When the pessimist sees difficulty in every opportunity, the optimist sees opportunity in every difficulty. That is me, an optimistic woman in all levels of my life.

I will always choose to be an optimist. Being strong is the only choice I have when I face difficulties. I can declare and decree anywhere I go. I have faith as a mustard seed that can move mountains. From the moment I discovered my purpose I felt free in my mind, spirit and soul. I believe the universe has plenty for everyone and me. All I have to do is to ask, and it shall be given to me, knock and it shall be opened for me. It is not luck, sorcery, or religion. It is my mustard-seed faith that I carry in my heart to make things happen for me at the right time and place. The world is my oyster; I have a Father in heaven who will never let me down, as long as He sits on His throne. I will never entertain the thought that my needs will not be met. His working power has been in motion since the day I was born, the day I survived all, and the day I gave my life to Him. He is everything to me. Surely, faith moves mountains. If you always envision the results at the end and trust your heart, it will lead straight to your destiny. I am alive and breathing. Nothing or no one, not even the devil in hell can stop my blessings or prevent me from reaching my destiny. Please do not give up yet, God is still in the business of miracles. I am a testimony and living proof. Trust me on this one.

Chapter 11

Conclusion
and Keys Takeaway

I want to say thank you to everyone who has read my story from the beginning until the end. When I first started thinking about writing this book, I never thought I would finish or even get so far. I postponed writing so many times, on top of not having a great laptop. It was old and frequently froze and blacked out when I was doing my writing. Sometimes I was so frustrated that I wanted to give up, but I am glad I did not. I would go to the library to continue writing.

However, one gladsome day, I felt inspired and wrote my first two chapters, and continued as the days, weeks, and months went by. I wrote the last two chapters at the start because those experiences were very fresh and new in my mind. So what is your excuse for not fulfilling your dreams and goals? If I can put my painful stories into writing an inspiring book, so can you. My parents always told me that I was a good writer. When I was in school, my writing always impressed my teachers and classmates. Writing has become my passion. Thanks to the pandemic which made me discover my passion and turn it into a purpose and a dream come true. I was afraid to put my life story out there. The world has now seen what I was in my past, and how far I have come to be where I am now and who I will become in my future. I love my privacy though, so not everything is shared. I do not want to be vulnerable to criticisms from my family, friends, or the society.

If my story will change the life of even one individual, or two on this planet, I would be happy. I am so glad that I faced my fears, which are made up of false evidence that appear to be real. At least, my talents and skills will not contribute to the wealth of the grave once I publish my book and touch many lives. I once heard a minister, I believe it was Myles Munroe, saying, "The wealthiest place on the planet is not in the Far East where there's oil in the ground, and it's not in South Africa where there are diamond mines. The wealthiest place on the planet is the cemetery. There you see potential never realized. There you find books never written. There you find ideas never acted on." I made a bold decision that my book will not be a part of the cemetery's wealth and so can you. I am not saying that you have to be a writer or follow the crowd. Your gifts want to be found. They want to be known and want to be friends with you, to shake your hands and say "Hello my friend, nice to finally meet you." Look deep inside of you, and you will find your gifts. They will become a passion that will turn into a purpose that will serve you for a lifetime. My deepest desire is to become an inspiration and a living testimony to humanity, especially women who are in deep despair.

This world is not getting better, people are scared of the world crisis and uncertainty of tomorrow. In the midst of this uncertainty, I want to become that love, faith, hope, strength, resilience, patience, compassion and kindness that the world needs now. You can become the change you want to see in the world. Become the change, the love and that beauty you want to see in the world. *Beauty begins the moment you decide to be yourself.---* Coco Chanel. There is an invisible dream waiting to be seen. People who cannot see your dream will never understand why you work so hard, why you spend time alone, why you become silent, and why you have no time for drama. Build in silence and one day your success will shock the whole world. You know what they will ask you: how did you do it? That is when your invisible dream makes a big noise of success. One final word: Jesus Christ is the answer to all the problems in this world, seek Him and you will find Him with all the blessings and treasures that you need. Do not look far away, He is right there by your side every single day when you are feeling hopeless, weak, anxious, fearful, depressed, lonely, or unlovable. Here is a promise given to us by God: *Fear not, for I am with you; Be not dismayed, for I am your God. I will strengthen you, Yes, I will help you. I will uphold you with my righteous right hand.*---Isaiah 41:10...DO NOT BE AFRAID is found 365 times in the Bible for you to remember each day of the year. Use it!